WHEN WE WERE FIFTY

Also by Christopher Matthew

WHEN WE WERE FIFTY
BY CHRISTOPHER MATTHEW
DECORATIONS BY DAVID ECCLES

JOHN MURRAY

For Grant McIntyre

First published in Great Britain in 2007 by John Murray (Publishers)
An Hachette Livre UK Company

1

Text © Christopher Matthew 2007

Illustrations © David Eccles 2007
(With sincere and affectionate tribute to the genius of Ernest Shepard)

The right of Christopher Matthew to be identified as the Author of the Work
has been asserted by him in accordance with the Copyright, Designs and
Patents Act 1988.

A CIP catalogue record for this title is available from the British Library

ISBN 978-0-7195-6885-5

Typeset in Goudy Old Style by
Palimpsest Book Production Limited, Grangemouth, Stirlingshire
Printed and bound by Butler & Tanner, Frome, Somerset

John Murray policy is to use papers that are natural, renewable and recyclable
products and made from wood grown in sustainable forests. The logging and
manufacturing processes are expected to conform to the environmental
regulations of the country of origin.

John Murray (Publishers)
338 Euston Road
London NW1 3BH

www.johnmurray.co.uk

INTRODUCTION

Noël Coward could always be depended upon to rustle up a bon mot or two on more or less any subject that came his way.

He was not a man much given to self-doubt – except on the subject of encroaching age.

On the occasion of his half-century he remarked, 'My body has certainly wandered a good deal these last 50 years, but I have the uneasy suspicion that my mind has not wandered nearly far enough.'

Lucky old so-and-so. All too many hit their 50ths feeling that, even in these days of cheap and easy air travel, their bodies have voyaged little further than their minds.

After years of being firmly anchored to hearth, home and the office computer by every imaginable responsibility that flesh is heir to – marital, financial, domestic and professional – they begin to wonder if the time has come to chuck in the humdrum life and strike out on their own.

They think of all the things they have dreamed of doing for decades, but which, for a variety of reasons, they have had to consign to the back shelf.

Could this be the moment, they ask themselves, to start living that dream – while they still have the time? After all, at 50 we're all a lot nearer the grave than the cradle.

Some sigh and shake their heads and carry on just as they are – in the same job, living in the same house, with the same wife, making more money, climbing towards even greater peaks. Bolder spirits seize the day and go for it.

Bank managers take up boat building; computer salesmen become film extras; a housewife enrols on a degree course in philosophy; a publisher learns to be a landscape gardener, or a rap artist.

At 50 the world can suddenly seem everyone's oyster. One is still young enough to rediscover long-forgotten pleasures. Men start second families; women re-start careers.

And then there are all those pleasures one has yet to experience, but now has the time – and the money – to try: living in a converted barn in the Auvergne; joining a bridge club; learning how to cook; acquiring a taste for opera; taking up hang-gliding; treating oneself to a grown-up gap year . . .

This little volume of verses – based, like *Now We Are Sixty* and *Now We Are Sixty (and a Bit)*, on the poems of A. A. Milne – has been written to celebrate that moment in life when men and women, bolstered by success, self-confidence, physical fitness and worldly wisdom, feel ready to grasp life by the scruff of the neck, give it a good shake and move serenely onwards into the sunny uplands of mature middle age.

CONTENTS

TIME WAS . . .
(*after* THE MORNING WALK)

At 50-ish my dear old Dad
Sat down and read the *Iliad*.
Like Priam, he had reached the stage
When men began to act their age.

But now I've hit the 50 mark,
Dad sounds like something from the ark.
I've better things to do all week
Than waste my time on some old Greek.

SIR JOHN'S PROBLEM
(*after* KING JOHN'S CHRISTMAS)

Sir John was quite an odd man
   In many, many ways,
And never quite so odd as in
   His old, pre-knighthood days.
Before he joined the great and good
   With entries in *Who's Who*,
He toiled as hard as anyone,
He'd never walk, but always run,
The workaholic No. 1—
   A slogger through and through.

That John was not a wise man;
   A gambler to his boots,
At work, at play, in every way,
   He took the gambler's routes.
His penchant was for poker
   And cards of every kind;
He'd work and play through all the year,
Then, bolstered up with Christmas cheer,
He'd pack his bags and disappear
   To Vegas and unwind.

He made a load of money
   When he was in his prime;
No sooner had he earned it than
   He lost it every time.
His wife was most forebearing,
   She rarely said a word;
She gardened hard and ran the house,
She didn't sulk, or bleat, or grouse;
She was for him the perfect spouse,
   Albeit wife the third.

Sir John was quite a kind man;
   He loved his little Kate,
And didn't want to see her hurt
   Or put her in a bate.
One year he had a brainwave—
   He clenched a trembling jaw,
And wrote to every gambling joint:
'I'm not a man to disappoint,
But if I turn up, make a point
   Of showing me the door.

11

'Ignore my protests,
    And refuse my bribes,
And turn the deafest ear you can
    To all my taunts and gibes.
I don't want arguments,
    I don't want fuss,
And I don't want violence,
    Or funny stuff. Plus,
Do me a favour, write a letter to my wife,
And tell her how I plan to lead a whole
    new kind of life.'

Sir John was quite romantic;
    He stood by the front door
And gathered up the letters as
    They fell upon the floor.
He wrapped them up in tissue,
    Went down on bended knee
Beside the bed on Christmas Day,
And handed Kate a silver tray,
And swore henceforth he'd never play:
    She had his guarantee.

'Forget about the poker,
    And forget about the debt;
From this time on, I'll never hold
    A card, or make a bet.
I don't need excitement,
    I don't want spice,
I've got a perfect marriage now
    With someone really nice.
So, here's my Christmas present: these letters
    from my clubs.
To prove how much I love you, Kate, I've
    cancelled all my subs.'

* * *

Sir John stood in his study
    And stared out at his lawn.
Resolve was weak; he cursed the day
    That ever he was born.
A letter from the taxman,
    The worst he'd ever seen,
Revealed he owed a dreadful sum;
His mind went blank, his brain was numb,
He scratched his nose, his ear, his bum,
    He hadn't got a bean.

Sir John was most resourceful;
    Within a week or less
He'd been to every gambling club
    To rectify the mess.
He tried out every cunning ruse,
    And every sort of spin—
Like dressing as an Arab sheik
In bedsheets that were clearly fake,
But no one made the daft mistake
    Of letting him come in . . .

* * *

Sir John kissed his beloved,
    And cut straight to the chase:
'We owe the taxman ninety grand,
    I fear I'm in disgrace.'
Kate said, 'We've got a problem;
    The bathroom man's an arse.
He's put the tiles on upside down,
They should be pale pink, not brown.
The man's a fool, a twerp, a clown—
    The whole thing looks a farce.'

Sir John was quite a calm man;
　He coughed and said, 'My dear,
You obviously weren't listening;
　You clearly didn't hear.
I said we owe a fortune . . .'
　She said, 'For all your wiles,
There's nothing you can do today,
There's nothing more to think or say,
So ring the man in Harringay,
　And sort these ruddy tiles.'

THE MORAL OF THIS STORY
　IS CLEAR TO ANY MAN:
　　　DON'T WASTE YOUR TIME
　　　WITH THINGS YOU CAN'T;
　　　GET ON WITH
　　　THINGS YOU CAN.

RESPECT
(*after* DAFFODOWNDILLY)

He wore a hooded sweatshirt,
   And jeans with pre-torn knees.
He cycled down the pavement
   As careless as you please.
I wore a tie and jacket,
   The trademarks of a toff.
I didn't have to say a word.
   I looked. He said, 'Fuck off!'

DECISIONS, DECISIONS
(*after* SPRING MORNING)

Where lies my future? I'm not quite sure.
I'm not all that rich, but I'd hate to be poor.
Should I stay as I am with my safe little life?
And my safe little job, and my safe little wife?

Or is 50 the moment to try something new
While my head is still clear and the skies are still blue?
I'm perfectly happy around Potters Bar,
But adventure still beckons; the door's still ajar.

What became of the dreams that I dreamed long ago
Of a life as a poet in old Mexico?
Or perhaps as the star of a string of stage hits?
Or just one of those fellows who live off their wits?

How *could* I have spent thirty years in those banks,
Changing pounds into dollars, and marks into francs?
Now the scales have been lifted, at last I can see
That from now on the thing that needs changing is me.

But what shall I do with the rest of my days?
I am spoilt for choice; I'm a man in a maze.
Should I start my own business, some sort of
    dot-com?
Or dream up the plot for a TV sitcom?

Retire to the country and start breeding pigs?
Become a film extra and wear silly wigs?
Disappear to Tahiti and paint lovely girls?
Set up shop in Damascus for gemstones and pearls?

When I spoke to my wife, she said, 'Don't talk
    such tripe.
You know you are not the adventurous type.
If you want some excitement, don't sit there and yawn.
Get out in the garden and mow the front lawn.'

YOU'RE NOT GOING OUT
IN THOSE?
(after BROWNIE)

In the corner of my wardrobe hung a pair of
    trousers
In lovely crushed blue velvet, with a medium flare.
I could still just have worn them (in a few friends'
    houses),
But sadly they're no longer there.

When I wasn't really looking, she threw them out
    as jumble.
She said, 'They're old and smelly, and they're
    out of date.'
My youth has gone for ever, but I shouldn't
    grumble—
In truth, I've put on quite a bit of weight.

WINNERS AND LOSERS
(after US TWO)

Wherever we went, there was always Doug;
There was always Doug and Dot.
I've never seen two looking quite so smug
When they won the heats of the jitterbug.
Dot looked like a very superior pug,
And Doug wore a smirk like I don't know what—
I wanted to punch his mug.

'Hearty congrats,' I said to Doug.
He smiled, the little snot,
And shook his head and shrugged a shrug,
And grabbed one ear and gave a tug.
He said, 'We cut a fairish rug.
Like some, we haven't lost the plot—
That way, you're down the plug.'

We went for a drink with Dot and Doug,
My partner Reg and me.
We gave them both a medium hug;
Doug looked as blank as a Toby jug;
Dot seemed as pleased as a warmed-up slug;
Reg swung his arms like a chimpanzee
Which has taken a class A drug.

We lost the finals to Doug and Dot,
When Reg did in his knee.
He said, 'To hell with this modern rot;
My cha-cha-cha has gone to pot.
The way things are going, our hopes are shot.
We're far better off in old Torquay,
Treading a light gavotte.'

Then Dot broke her toe with a coffee pot,
And Reg developed a pile.
Doug said, 'Your chap is in a spot.
I reckon we'd be hot to trot
In the National Finals in Aldershot.
Dot is off games for quite some while,
So why not give it a shot?'

Now wherever I go, there's always Doug;
There's always Doug and me.
I learnt Dot's moves in the jitterbug,
And we won the Jerry Lee Lewis Mug.
On the floor we're as snug as a socket and plug
(Some might say as a pod and pea),
And, frankly, I'm feeling quite smug.

MEMORY LANE
(*after* MARKET SQUARE)

I got a letter,
A nice typed letter,
Signed by a fellow
  Who was in 3B,
Inviting me to come to
A class reunion—
'It's just a jolly social,
  A bit of fun.'

So I went to the place which I call my alma mater.
(*Nice old buildings, royal charter.*)
I looked for some school chums, like Smith and Jones
    and Carter,
  But I didn't know a soul there, not a single one.

I got a phone call,
A nice long phone call;
A friend of mine,
     Where I used to live,
Wanted me to come to
A 50th party—
'And have a little wander
     Down memory lane.'

So I went to the place where I lived with my family.
(*Nice neat cul-de-sac, well-clipped hedges.*)
I looked for some faces that I knew from my salad days,
     But every single one of them had moved to Spain.

I got an e-mail,
A chatty little e-mail;
It came from a bloke
   Where I used to work:
Any chance at all I was
Free next week for
An office get-together—
   Just a few old mates?

So I went to the place where I worked in finance.
(Nice big office block, much refurbished.)
But hard though I hunted for a glimpse of my glory days,
   All I saw were pimply youths and dull featherweights.

I got a message,
A mystic message;
It came to me one morning
   Around half past four:
Ignore all letters
And phone calls and e-mails,
Inviting me to re-live
   My days of yore.

I'm sorry for my chums who go to reunions;
I'm sorry for my friends who have 50th parties;
I'm sorry for my mates in their dull old offices;
   For nothing in one's past is as it was before.

SATISFACTION
(*after* SOLITUDE)

I have a chair where I sit
   At the end of a table.
This is the place where I fit,
   And no one but me.
Shareholders vote me a hit;
Others here think I'm a twit;
But, frankly, I don't give a shit—
   'Cos I'm the chairman, see?

INSURANCE RISK
(*after* TWINKLETOES)

When our son
Drives through the gates of our Surrey home;
When our child
Scrapes the wing, the bumper and the polished chrome;
There I stand,
Head in hand.
I try hard not to worry;
That's life for you—in Surrey.
I know, I know . . .
It's only money.

FAT
(after HAPPINESS)

Ron had
A gut
The size of an
Airship.
Ron's bum was
Wider
Than the M
25.
Ron was a
Bachelor
And lived on
Sausages,
And lucky
To be
    A-
     live.

TALK THE TALK
(*after* THE KNIGHT WHOSE ARMOUR DIDN'T SQUEAK)

Of all the men in marketing,
  The saddest was Llewellyn Leek.
He never said a single thing
  Unless in new-style office speak.
He lived near Sevenoaks in Kent,
And looked a bit like David Brent.

He left for work at six fifteen;
　By seven he was at his desk,
In front of his computer screen.
　His working life was quite grotesque.
He had no time to hob or nob;
The whole day he was on the job.

He never paused to clear his mind,
　Or have a chat, or crack a joke.
He deskfasted and dashboard-dined;
　He wasn't like a normal bloke.
While friends were having lunch al fresco,
He ate his sandwiches al desko.

He'd kick dead whales down the beach,
    And knife and fork a tricky task,
And bandy words like infospeech—
    Though what they meant few dared to ask.
He'd magpie this and wild card that,
And eat his own dog food—and cat.

His whole life was informed by dread
    He might commit a CLM.
'Don't miss a trick or lose your head'
    Was his abiding apothegm.
One slip and he'd be on his way,
And end up with a salmon day.

An ideas hamster marked his card:
   'A light-bulb moment's what you need;
Just push the peanut forward hard.
   Appeal to their sense of greed.
There's nothing pleases IICs
Like Bernies earned with careless ease.'

So when the light bulb flashed, he tried
    His idea on the IICs.
They killed it with vanillacide,
    And turned deaf ears to all his pleas.
And no one dared to shoot the pup,
So, just like that, his time was up.

Now Llew is very nicely wedged,
    With schools on both sides of the pond,
Where quite big cheeses, it's alleged,
    Flock in from hither and beyond,
And leave—sometimes within a week—
Fluent in new office speak.

Deskfast: eat breakfast at your desk.

Dashboard dining: eating dinner in your car.
Otherwise known as *à la car.*

Kick dead whales down the beach: take on an
unpleasant and interminable task.

Knife and fork it: deal with a problem bit by bit.

Infospeech: I made it up.

Magpie: possibly to steal other people's ideas,
though I may have made this up too.

Wild carding: suggesting to your client your
favourite solutions, plus a couple of other
wackier possibilities.

Dog food: cheap product for the masses.

CLM: career-limiting move.

Salmon day: one in which you swim upstream all
day, only to be thoroughly shafted at the end
of it.

Ideas hamster: one who, as a result of some good
light-bulb moments, has waved goodbye to his
low-grade life as a cubicle monkey.

Push the peanut: give one's little grey cells a good
workout.

IICs: idiots in charge.

Bernie: £1 million, named after Bernie Ecclestone
who offered £1 million to the Labour Party.

Vanillacide: destroying good ideas with too much
discussion.

Shoot the pup: dare to do the unthinkable.

Wedged: rich

ADVENTURE
(*after* THE FRIEND)

There are lots and lots of places I've not had time
   to see,
Like Angkor Wat, the Barrier Reef, and Rio, and
   Fiji.
I'd love to trek to Lhasa, and swim with tiger
   sharks,
And wear sarongs, and bungee jump, and other
   silly larks.

It's time I took a gap year and had a bit of fun,
And set off with a rucksack in search of sex and
  sun . . .
I don't know quite what happened, it's all there in
  my head,
Yet here I am in Oslo on a Saga cruise instead.

THE DOWNSHIFTER
(*after* THE ENGINEER)

Stuff careers!
What glee!
Three cheers,
I'm free!
Screw the suits,
I wear boots,
Caked with mud,
Crap and crud . . .
Four-by-four,
Filled with straw,
Parked outside
The kitchen door.
New bride,
Labrador,
Ten brown cows,
Sheep in pens,
Free-range hens,
Six plump sows . . .

Farewell, funds,
Clever hunches,
Business lunches,
Cummerbunds . . .

Downshifting's the thing.
Some think I'm a twit,
But my heartstrings go zing,
Like a pig's in shit.

EX-PAT
(*after* THE OLD SAILOR)

There was once an accountant called Bill from East
   Cheam,
Who for years had been dreaming a glorious dream
That somehow one day through hard work, or pure
   chance,
He would set himself up in a villa in France.

> He was bored with the blokes that he met in the pub;
> He was bored with the beer and bored with the grub;
> He was tired of the jokes that he heard on the train;
> He was tired of the cold, and tired of the rain.

He pictured a rather more civilized life
(And, if he was honest, a quite different wife),
And elegant parties, with real caviare,
By a pool with a view of St Jean-Cap Ferrat.

So he worked every hour that the Lord had bestowed,
But search as he might for the Yellow Brick Road,
All he met was a mountain of statements and bills,
With no sign at all of those sun-dappled hills.

And the voices around him grew ever more coarse
(And his wife had begun to resemble a horse),
And the 6.54 had a curious knack
Of a daily encounter with leaves on the track . . .

Then one day in April the telephone rang,
And he learnt of the death of an aunt in Penang,
Who had left all her money, divided in ten,
Between him and his cousins and big sister, Gwen.

So, if not quite a villa, the sun, or the Med,
He could stretch to a broken-down farmhouse
    instead
In a little-known region just north of the Var,
Only twenty-two hours from Surrey by car.

And he did the place up with a builder from Kew
With a very posh voice and a shaved head, called
  Hugh,
Who created a look which he called 'rustic chic',
Which was basically French, with a slight hint of
  Greek.

Each evening at seven, Bill got in his car
And he drove down the hill and he sat in the bar,
Where he ate a few snails and drank pastis galore,
With no loud English voices to stick in his craw.

But then Bill lost his head and the silly old berk
Got a flash English glossy to feature Hugh's work.
And before you could say 'Terence Conran' and
  curse,
The whole place was crawling with Cheamites, and
  worse.

And the bar started serving *le afternoon tea*,
And its atmosphere reeked of a film by Mike Leigh,
And the drink of the house became Stella on draught,
And the English who tried to speak French
  sounded daft.

So Bill sold up in France and he moved in with Hugh
In a French-style cottage in rustic-chic Kew,
Where they sit in LE BAR and drink pastis galore,
And now Bill never thinks about France any more.

SUSPICION
(*after* MISSING)

Has anybody seen my spouse?

He left for the office at seven forty,
(And told me a joke which was rather naughty).
He said he'd be home about half past eight,
And he'd ring if he thought he was going to be late.
I really don't want to appear to grouse—
Has *anyone* seen my spouse?

Where the hell has he got to, my spouse?

He's a mild-mannered sort and not wildly sexy;
The mere word 'affair' would induce apoplexy.
But he talks a great deal about Jill, his assistant,
And he isn't the type to be firmly resistant.

He mentioned a meeting; it could be code
For the start of a trip down the rockiest road . . .

He should be home soon,
The silly baboon . . .

Has *anybody* seen my spouse?

FEELING YOUR AGE
(*after* DAFFODOWNDILLY)

He wore his green bermudas,
  He wore a stupid hat;
Across his purple tee shirt
  Were the words 'THIS MAN'S A PRAT'.

He says, 'I'm feeling 20,
  I thought I'd have a laugh.'
Next thing he knows, he's hooked up to
  An electrocardiograph.

D-A-A-AD!
(after JONATHAN JO)

If I try a bon mot,
My kids shout, 'Oh no!'
And my jokes are as a flat as a pancake.
If we're driving along
And I burst into song,
I'm pulled up by a sharp vocal handbrake.

If I mention 'the scene',
  And enthuse about Queen
And the days of 'Bohemian Rhapsody',
  They just all roll their eyes
  And emit groans and sighs,
And play music that sounds like sheer crap to me.

At my 50th bash
   I made quite a splash
With my white-suited nod to the Bee Gees.
   The kids turned bright red
   And went straight home to bed—
But my pals reckoned I was the bee's knees.

MASCULINITY
(*after* HOPPITY)

My silly husband goes
'Fuckity, fuckity
Fuckity, fuckity, fuck.'
If ever I ask him politely to chuck it, he
Puts on a sad show of pluck.

He's perfectly hopeless with hammer and nail, and
Tries DIY like
A typical male, and
Always ends up going
'Fuckity, fuckity,
Fuckity,
Fuckity,
Fuck.'

COLD CALLING
(*after* THE FRIEND)

There are lots and lots of people who are always
    on the phone,
With sing-song Asian accents and a rather
    smarmy tone.
They always want to sell me things I never want
    to buy—
Like mobile phones and timeshare homes and
    broadband deals and Sky.

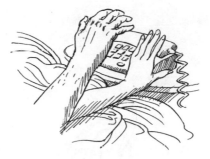

They always choose a rotten time, like half past
    ten at night,
Or when I'm having Sunday lunch and feeling
    slightly tight.
I'd really like to help them 'cos I know they're
    very poor,
But how I wish they'd find another job in
    Bangalore.

MID-LIFE CRISIS
(*after* RICE PUDDING)

What is the matter with Andrew Kane?
He's wearing those stupid clothes again,
And smirking like mad at his secretary, Jane—
Oh, isn't the middle-age crisis a pain?

The brightest of men seem bereft of a brain,
And the stupidest think they're the next Michael
   Frayn,
And bald-headed twerps become dreadfully vain,
And grow huge moustaches like Saddam Hussein.

The unlikeliest types get a taste for cocaine,
And yachts and Ferraris and villas in Spain,
And starting the day with a glass of champagne,
And learning to cook and to fly a light plane.

Their attempts to join in with the young are inane;
They make fools of themselves and they think
   they're urbane,
And they tell silly jokes and then laugh like a
   drain,
And think they're as sexy as old Michael Caine.

To their friends they become an impossible bane,
And about as amusing as old-style Sinn Fein,
And often more moody than Hamlet the Dane—
Does middle-age angst have to be *such* a pain?

IF ONLY . . .
(*after* AT HOME)

I want a facelift
(A bloody good facelift);
I want a surgeon who nips and tucks and tweaks.
I'd give a fortune
(Cash down, no prob)
For eyes without crows' feet and soft, smooth cheeks.

I want a tummy job
(Lipo, big time);
I want a midriff like a model on the telly.
But I'm nearly 50
And a lady who lunches,
And drinks a bit and has a fatal taste for pappardelle.

UPGRADING
(*after* THE WRONG HOUSE)

We had this little house, this very nice house,
  With three small beds and a farm-style kitch;
But it hadn't got a garden—
          Just a tiny
          Patio;
  In fact, it was all too titch.

So we borrowed to the hilt and we gave the place
a lift,
With all new carpets and some Ashley prints;
And we added a bathroom—
Quality
Marble,
Off-white with Tuscan tints.

Then we sold our little house, and we bought
another house—
Double-fronted, half a mile away;
And it had a lovely garden—
Big lawn,
Fishpond,
And a flat where Granny could stay.

We loved our nice new house, our grown-up house,
  With its garden, its games room and its granny flat;
But we didn't like our bathroom—
            Pink tiles,
            Gold taps,
  And flying ducks—a load of tat.

We went past our old house, our nice little house;
  The builders were in, with a big yellow skip;
And in it was our bathroom—
            Our brand new
            Bathroom,
  Ready to be taken to the tip.

71

So we hired a little van, a nice little van,
   And we drove round the corner in the dead of night;
And we loaded up our bathroom—
          Our marble
          Bathroom,
   Gleaming in the pale moonlight.

And it fitted like a dream in our nice new house,
   And we saved a fortune, just as they'd have done;
But they're investment bankers—
          Dirt rich
          Wankers;
   And just for once we feel we've won.

NEGATIVE EQUITY
(*after* IN THE FASHION)

My daughter is in debt, and my son, and his mate;
They all have overdrafts and, sad to relate,
Most of their friends have a bank to placate—
    They've been on a spending spree.

If I were a rich man, I could save them;
I'd pay back the money that the banks all gave them;
I'd help them to loosen the chains that enslave
them—
In one bound they'd be free.

What I'm tempted to say is, 'Let's end this charade
Of pretending that life for the young is so hard.
Stop living on credit and cut up your card.'
But how can I? They're richer than me.

MUTTON AND LAMB
(*after* THE DORMOUSE AND
THE DOCTOR)

There was a divorcée of 50 called Lou,
Who habitually dressed in light brown and dark blue.
She looked like a woman whom life had let down,
In her jumpers (dark blue) and her cardies (light
    brown).

In her 20s she'd been a real stunner, they said;
When she walked down the street she turned
    everyone's head.
Her skirts were as mini as mini could be,
And her bust (always bra-less) was 34C.

Her favourite colour was pillarbox red
(Though she tried lots of others at home, and in bed),
But wherever she went, in the country or town,
She never wore blue and she never wore brown.

In her 30s and 40s she looked half her age—
So much so, she quite lost her head at one stage.
She had shoulder-length hair, which she wore in a
    snood,
And her skirts were so short they were, frankly,
    quite rude.

But her legs, which had once been the talk of the town
(And, whatever the season, were beautifully brown),
Began to resemble a Danish blue cheese,
With the veins on her thighs and the backs of her
    knees.

And havoc was wrought on her bust and her bum
(For when gravity rules, all must one day succumb);
And, as 50 approached and her waist slowly spread,
She began to feel oddly imperfect in red.

Her daughters said, 'Mum, you are middle-aged now,
And you don't want to look like an overdressed cow.'
So, from that moment on, and without more ado,
She began to wear nothing but brown and dark blue.

She decided that glamour and sex were a bore,
And battling nature each day was a chore.
So, rather than end up like Bonzo the clown,
She'd wear cardies (dark blue) and big jumpers
   (light brown),

And Jesus-type sandals and frocks big as tents,
Bought from second-hand shops for a handful of pence.
She abandoned all semblance of style and taste,
With a twinset and skirt with adjustable waist.

Her once long, blonde hair was a grizzly frizz;
She wore two silly plaits and she called herself 'Ms'.
She never used lipstick, or make-up at all;
In a bad light she looked just like Asterix the Gaul.

A friend said, 'You're mad; you've no need to give in
Just because you're no longer as thin as a pin.
At 50 you know how to dress at your best,
So have confidence—give all that brown stuff a rest.

'You're no longer young, but you're surely not old.
Seize the moment! Go for it! Be daring! Be bold!
Think Duchess of Cornwall, think sexy, think
      you—
And you'll never again dress in light brown or
      blue.'

So she pulled up her socks and she shopped till
      she dropped,
And the next time they saw her, her daughters'
      eyes popped.
And she married a prince with a castle in Spain,
And she never wore light brown or dark blue again.

So, if ever you're tempted to chuck in the towel,
And hide under clothes that are fusty and foul,
Think of Lou in her cardies and jumpers and stuff,
And, like her, tell yourself, 'That's enough!' And be tough.

THE EMPTY NEST
(*after* DOWN BY THE POND)

I'm thinking.
Don't call, anybody, don't ring my phone.
Can't you see I must be alone?
The house is empty, it's terribly sad;
The silence is quite frightening, I think I'm going mad.
I feel my spirits sinking;
I've got to do some thinking.
So that's what I'm doing—
Thinking.

No, no, I'm not sulking.
Don't speak, anybody, I'm not at my best.
The last duckling's fled the familial nest.
I sat there at dinner last night and thought 'Wow!
It looks as if we'll have to reinvent our lives—but how?'
I promise I'm not sulking;
It could be that I'm skulking.
Yes, that's what I'm doing—
Skulking.

PROSPECTS
(*after* HALFWAY DOWN)

Halfway through my life
I'm as fit
As a flea.
I know a lot of
Other blokes
Just like
Me.
We know we're not kids, yet
We're now at the stage
When we've got more snap
Than
Chaps half our
Age.

Midway on the waves
I'm as strong
As an ox.
At 80-something kilos
I'm six foot in my socks.
I run five miles every day,
I don't drink or smoke—
I'll live to be
A hundred,
Somewhere nice, like
Basingstoke.

EVENING CLASSES
(*after* CHERRY STONES)

Shorthand typing,
Chinese juggling,
Cake decoration,
Web design.

And what about astronomy,
Tai chi, yoga,
Ancient history,
Or vintage wine?

What about flamenco, or creating silly hats?
What about clay modelling, or breeding Persian cats?
Or basic taxidermy, say, or making smelly cheese?
Or learning how to lag your loft, or amateur striptease?

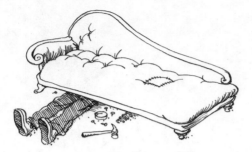

What about upholstery? First steps in reflexology?
What about philately—or other sorts of -ology?
Oh, there's such a lot of catching up for chaps my
    age to do,
But as for where to start, I simply haven't got a clue.

RABBITING ON
(*after* SHOES AND STOCKINGS)

There's a loggia in our semi where our book club
    meets.
(*Rabbit, rabbit, rabbit . . .*
Rabbit, rabbit, rabbit . . .)
We all read everything and no one cheats.
(*Rabbit, rabbit, rabbit . . .*
Rabbit, rabbit, rabbit . . .)

We tried Claire Tomalin, and Paul Theroux,
And nice John Updike, who was rather blue;
But Jeffrey and Joanna are our secret treats.
Rabbit, rabbit, rabbit . . .
Rabbit . . .

87

There's a table in our kitchen where our prayer group
  sits.
(*Murmur, murmur, murmur . . .*
Murmur, murmur, murmur . . .)
The two who run it are a pair of twits.
(*Murmur, murmur, murmur . . .*
Murmur, murmur, murmur . . .)
I don't mind giving thanks for God's good air,
Or even (if I must) our kitchen chair;
But praying for this government is just the pits.
Murmur, murmur, murmur . . .
Murmur . . .

SUNDAY SPORT
(*after* WAITING AT THE WINDOW)

These are my two favourite men:
One's called Bill and one's called Ben.

It's Sunday morning in the park,
And, being winter, rather dark.

A rugger game is under way—
My two, as always, in the fray.

Bill's team is pushing well ahead;
Ben's could have stayed at home in bed.

Bill on his own has scored four tries;
He's getting lots of exercise.

Bill's knees are white as driven snow—
Ben's caked in mud from top to toe.

Bill takes a pass, he's on the charge;
Compared with Ben, he's awfully large.

The try-line looms, there's no defence;
Then Ben appears—he stands there, tense.

He hurls himself at Bill's white knees;
It's Tom Thumb versus Hercules!

Ben ends up, winded, in the mire,
Feeling like a punctured tyre.

Bill grounds the ball and punches air;
Poor Ben can only sit and stare.

The whistle goes, the dads have won.
Bill says to Ben, 'Now listen, son,

'Remember, next time tackle low,
And go for it like billy-o.

'Be more like me, no ifs and buts,
Just get stuck in and show some guts.'

> A man is always hard to beat,
> Who cannot play and not compete.

> And thinks that there's no greater fun
> Than beating his small schoolboy son.

Loadsamoney

THOSE WERE THE DAYS
(*after* KNIGHTS AND LADIES)

When I am wide awake in bed,
I sometimes make an A to Z
Of all the things that changed our lives
When we were young and had no wives;
When Mrs T. was in her prime,
And Robin Day did *Question Time*—
Laptops, Big Bang, fax machines,
One pound coins, designer jeans;
Sony Walkmans, compact discs,
Stand-up comics who took risks;
Amber nectar, Sky TV,
Bottled water, Ecstasy;
Filofaxes, kiwi fruit,
Glasnost and the yuppy suit;
Star Wars, spritzers, Channel 4,
Making money, more and more;
The eighties were the days, my friend,
We hoped—and thought—they'd never end.
But HIV knocked all that flat,
And Thatcher went, and that was that.

TIME OF OUR LIVES
(*after* TWICE TIMES)

There were two 50-somethings who lived on a hill,
And one of them was Jaz and the other was Jill.
Jill had a face like a cross pork pie,
But Jaz—she had looks for which women would die.

They'd met in the dorm on their first day at school—
A Victorian pile to the north of Goole.
Jill harboured dreams of becoming a nun,
But Jaz went to bed with the art master's son.

Jaz took to drugs and went round in a trance,
And married a Greek in the South of France.
Jill got a job serving soup to the poor,
And gave up religion and married a bore.

Jaz lived in Capri, Barbados and Spain,
And married for money again and again.
She spent a small fortune on treatments and spas,
And spent even more in smart nightclubs and bars.

Jill stayed at home and looked after her brood;
She ironed lots of shirts and she cooked lots of food.
She struggled with homework—they mostly had tons—
And measured her life out in endless school runs.

Now Jaz lives near Jill on the top of a hill,
In a one-bedroom flat with a fellow called Bill.
She lost all her money, she's losing her looks,
And she hasn't got children, just boxes of books.

There may be a moral—although maybe not—
About what you are born with and what you have got.
Some people may talk of the tortoise and hare,
And which of the two did what, why and where.
But the fact is, in springtime, none of us knows
How cookies crumble and where the wind blows.

LATE DEVELOPER
(*after* WIND ON THE HILL)

Everyone tells me,
   Everyone knows,
Culture's the thing now,
   So that's what I chose.

I went to the Garden
   To see *Cav* and *Pag*—
To tell you the truth,
   It was rather a drag.

I tried to get keen
   On contemporary art—
I honestly couldn't
   Have given a fart.

I sat through a concert
  Of *musique concrète*—
I wasn't the only one
  Snoring, I'll bet.

I thought I should try
  The *Macbeth* from Zaire—
By the time I came out,
  I felt older than Lear.

For me, I'm afraid
  Art's a terrible waste—
To be perfectly frank,
  I'm a man with no taste.

MARRIAGE
(*after* A THOUGHT)

If I were you and you were me,
You'd be at work and I'd be free.
If you were me and I were you,
I'd bugger off to Kathmandu.

MATURE STUDENT
(*after* PINKLE PURR)

Susanne was the mother of Jacqueline—
The prettiest girl that you've ever seen.
Dear Suse had once been a beauty, like her,
But life had shot by in a glamorous blur.
So, when J. went to Oxford at sweet seventeen,
Mum couldn't resist being part of the scene.

She'd arrive without warning and chat up the blokes,
And embarrass poor J. with unsuitable jokes,
And drink cheap champagne and get drunk in a punt,
And show off her legs at the back—and the front—
And watch the bumps races* and cheer on the strokes,†
And bang on their doors when they'd sported their
    oaks.‡

She became a familiar face in the quads,
And went to some lectures on Greece and its Gods,
And when J. asked the porter to not let her in,
She went home with the porter and lived there in sin.
Now Jacqui is living abroad with odd bods,
And her mother has just got a First in her Mods.§

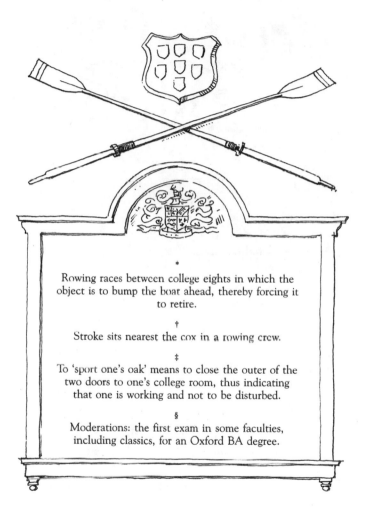

Rowing races between college eights in which the object is to bump the boat ahead, thereby forcing it to retire.

†

Stroke sits nearest the cox in a rowing crew.

‡

To 'sport one's oak' means to close the outer of the two doors to one's college room, thus indicating that one is working and not to be disturbed.

§

Moderations: the first exam in some faculties, including classics, for an Oxford BA degree.

BALDNESS BE MY FRIEND
(*after* SAND-BETWEEN-THE-TOES)

I went round to the unisex—
Salon des maîtres (with circumflex).
My dome is bald, with a fuzzy rim,
But I still pop in for a trim.

  I've got hair on my legs and my bum and my
    toes,
  And hair on my chin, in my ears, up my nose;
  I've got hair everywhere that a man's hair grows,
  But my scalp's something else—
  It's a *quelquechose*.

My dad was a slaphead at 28;
Trichologically speaking, that settled my fate.
My schoolfriends were mopheads, like young Tony
  Blair;
As for me—you'd have thought Clement Attlee
  was there.

I had hair on my thighs, on my tum, on my rear;
And hair on my hands, on my cheeks, in each ear;
Not for nothing was I the King Kong of my year,
But my bonce was as smooth
As the finest cashmere.

In my 20s and 30s I tried every trick
To conceal the fact that I looked like a dick.
But now that I'm 50, no one can scoff,
'Cos I've shaved the whole lot off.

And I look just as young as my friends
    who've got hair
On their heads, on their arms, in their ears,
    everywhere.
I may look like a robber, a skinhead, a thug,
But I'd rather look scary
Than wear a brown rug.

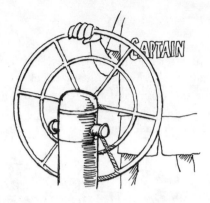

THE LEAD IN THE
BOXING GLOVE
(after GROWING UP)

I've got a bloody good personal trainer;
I've got a wife like Mitzi Gaynor;
I'm good looking and I entertain her—
  Who's doing better than me?

I've got a place on the French Riviera;
I've got a yacht called *Habanera*;
I heli-ski in the High Sierra—
  Who's doing better than me?

*   *   *

I've had a note from the bank's big cheeses;
Seems I'm the victim of one of their squeezes.
When they get a cold, then somebody sneezes—
Who's doing better? Not me!

TENTH COMMANDMENT
(*after* IN THE FASHION)

My neighbour has a Rolls and a Jag like Morse;
His wife has a Jeep and a box for her horse;
His daughter's got a Golf—GT, of course,
    And I've got an old MG.

If I were a banker, I'd have a Ferrari;
I'd drive with the top down and look pretty starry;
I'd take all the family away on safari,
    Instead of to Leigh-on-Sea.

But I'm just a vicar without any money;
My wife is a nurse and an absolute honey;
We don't go abroad, but our life's always sunny,
    And nobody envies me!

INVISIBLE
(*after* BEFORE TEA)

Geoffrey Dean
Has not been seen
For over a year; he disappeared
One day in the street, it was really weird;
It was as if he had never been.

Two young things—
Long legs on springs—
Came bouncing past him one summer's day.
He smiled at them both in a nice, friendly way.
They never saw.
Poor Geoffrey thought 'Lor!'

In middle age
We all reach a stage
When we suddenly know that we're no longer there.
Our storehouse of youth and good looks is quite bare.
Where has he gone,
That glorious swan?
He's there just as much as he's always been,
That debonair charmer called Geoffrey Dean.
To the young, though, such notions are faintly
    obscene.

SECOND FATHERHOOD
(after VESPERS)

Oliver kneels on the wet bathroom floor;
Wipes his wet hands on his wet pinafore—
Splish! Splash! 'Isn't this fun?'
Middle-aged daddy is bathing his son.

My friends think I'm mad to have started again;
I was never the most baby-minded of men.
I was rarely around when the first brood were
    small,
And the day they were born I was not there at all.

Number four, I'll admit, was a bit of a bish,
On account of the fact that my new wife's a dish.
But, like Humphrys and Jason and Stewart and
    Brown,*
I am aiming to be the best father in town.

I'm a dab hand at nappies and bottles and teats,
And walks on the common and other such treats.
It's great being fluent in gobbledygook,
And I love going round smelling faintly of puke.

* John Humphrys, broadcaster; Sir David Jason, actor; Rod
Stewart, singer; Gordon Brown, politician. All fathers in late
middle age.

I know that my first wife would call me a freak;
The older ones swear they can hear my bones creak.
The fact of the matter is—hip, hip, hooray!—
Yesterday's 30 is 50 today.

Oliver sits by the Mothercare cot;
Rubs his sore knees and massages his pot;
Smiles, sighs—'Wasn't that fun!'
Middle-aged dad says goodnight to his son.

ON THE TOWN
(*after* SWING SONG)

Here I am, 50 today.
    Wa'hey!
Drinking champagne with my pals, after work
    In the pub;
Chucking myself around with some girl
    In a club.
I'm a lad. 50 today?
    No way!